Platypus & Echidna

My First Picture Book

Steve Parish
PUBLISHING
www.steveparish.com.au

Platypuses and echidnas belong to a group of animals called mammals.

They are different from other mammals because their babies hatch from eggs.

Mammals that lay eggs are called monotremes.

An echidna eats termites and ants. It uses its long, sticky tongue to lick them up.

An echidna's back is covered in sharp spines. Fur grows between the spines.

A baby echidna stays in its burrow until its spines are grown.

An echidna rolls itself into a spiky ball when it is frightened.

Sometimes an echidna might use its sharp claws to dig into the ground to hide.

Platypuses live near clear, running water. They dig a burrow in the bank of a creek.

A platypus has thick, waterproof fur, and a broad, rubbery bill.

It feeds on small creatures it finds in the mud on the creek-bed or under rocks.

When a platypus swims underwater, it shuts its eyes, ears and nostrils.

A platypus has webbed feet. It uses its fore feet to swim and hind feet to steer.

Echidnas are good swimmers too.

platypus

echidna